FAMILIES JUST LIKE MINE (ONLY DIFFERENT)

Written by Eliza Nodes

KidHaven PUBLISHING

Published in 2026 by
KidHaven Publishing, an Imprint of Greenhaven Publishing, LLC
2544 Clinton St., Buffalo, NY 14224

Written by: Eliza Nodes
Edited by: Rebecca Phillips-Bartlett
Designed by: Amelia Harris

All facts, statistics, web addresses, and URLs in this book were verified as valid and accurate at time of writing. No responsibility for any changes to external websites or references can be accepted by either the author or publisher.

Cataloging-in-Publication Data

Names: Nodes, Eliza.
Title: Families / Eliza Nodes.
Description: Buffalo, NY : KidHaven Publishing, 2026. | Series: Just like mine (only different) | Includes glossary and index.
Identifiers: ISBN 9781534551640 (pbk.) | ISBN 9781534551657 (library bound) | ISBN 9781534551664 (ebook)
Subjects: LCSH: Families--Juvenile literature.
Classification: LCC HQ744.N634 2026 | DDC 306.85--dc23

Printed in China

CPSIA compliance information: Batch #QW26KH: For further information contact Greenhaven Publishing LLC at 1-844-317-7404.

Please visit our website, www.greenhavenpublishing.com.
For a free color catalog of all our high-quality books, call toll free 1-844-317-7404 or fax 1-844-317-7405.

Find us on

Image Credits

Images courtesy of Shutterstock.com, unless otherwise stated.
Recurring – 501room, Irina Strelnikova. Cover – Oksana Kuzmina, John Kasawa, Lopolo, Monsterstock, fast-stock, szefei, PeopleImages.com - Yuri A, 3d_hokage. 2–3 – Drazen Zigic. 4–5 – GillianVann, Monkey Business Images. 6–7 – Monkey Business Images. 8–9 – PeopleImages.com - Yuri A. 10–11 – all_about_people, SeventyFour. 12–13 – StockImageFactory.com. 14–15 – Monsterstock. 16–17 – fizkes, Anna Bova. 18–19 – PeopleImages.com - Yuri A. 20–21 – SurfsUp, Okrasiuk. 22–23 – Pixel-Shot, Jackson Stock Photography.

CONTENTS

WORDS THAT LOOK LIKE THIS CAN BE FOUND IN THE GLOSSARY ON PAGE 24.

A LOOK AROUND THE SCHOOL FAIR

This weekend, my school is having a summer fair. Everyone from school brings their families to have fun and support the school.

A family is a group of people who are connected by ancestry, love, or another strong bond. It is so nice to see my friends' families at the school fair.

MY FAMILY

This is my family. I live with my mom, my dad, and my little brother. My mom's name is Monica. My dad's name is Andrew. I love them both a lot!

My little brother is named Daniel. I love him too. I love spending time with my family. We play sports together!

JACKSON'S FAMILY

My friend Jackson lives with his dad and younger brother. Jackson's dad is a single parent. This means he is the only parent taking care of Jackson most of the time.

Jackson's mom and dad are separated. Jackson was sad when his parents first separated, but he loves seeing his mom on weekends. They do lots of fun things together.

SERI'S FAMILY

My friend Seri has two dads. Their names are Jae and Seok. She calls Jae Daddy, and she calls Seok Papa. They all like to read together.

On Father's Day, Seri makes one card for each of her dads. Father's Day is a special day for Seri and her dads. They play games together and cook their favorite foods for dinner.

ARJUN'S FAMILY

Arjun lives with his mom, dad, big sister, and grandparents. Arjun's relatives are all very close and help one another. Arjun's parents find it easier to help Arjun's grandparents because they all live together.

Arjun's family are Hindu. Family is very important in Hinduism. Arjun's parents take the responsibility of looking after their parents very seriously. Arjun and his family celebrate Hindu festivals together.

BELLA'S FAMILY

Bella lives with her mom and dad. Her dad is transgender. This means that when he was born, the doctors said he was a girl, but he identifies as a man.

Bella loves bringing her parents to the fair. Her mom and dad are amazing at the ring toss game. One of their favorite family activities is going to carnivals and playing the games there.

VIOLET'S FAMILY

My friend Violet's family is a blended family. A blended family is two families coming together to make one family. Violet's dad married someone who was not Violet's mom, so now Violet has a stepmom.

Violet's stepmom had a daughter before she married Violet's dad. She is Violet's stepsister. Violet loves her stepmom and stepsister. Violet's stepmom helps her with her homework.

LOGAN'S FAMILY

Some of my friends are adopted. This means their parents did not give birth to them, but they are their legal parents. My friend Logan was adopted by his moms.

LOGAN'S MOMS ARE NAMED TARA AND CLAIRE.

Before he was adopted, Logan's moms were his foster parents. He lived with them, but they were not his legal parents yet. Foster parents care for kids whose birth parents can't care for them.

MASON'S FAMILY

Mason's mom is a single mom. She decided to have a baby without a partner. Doctors helped Mason's mom get pregnant. Mason's mom loves him very much.

Mason and his mom love gardening together. Mason's aunt helps them too! They grow vegetables in their garden. Mason's mom cuts their homegrown carrots into sticks.

END OF THE SCHOOL FAIR

It is time for the school fair to end. Everyone showed up to support the school. It was great to see my friends and their families today.

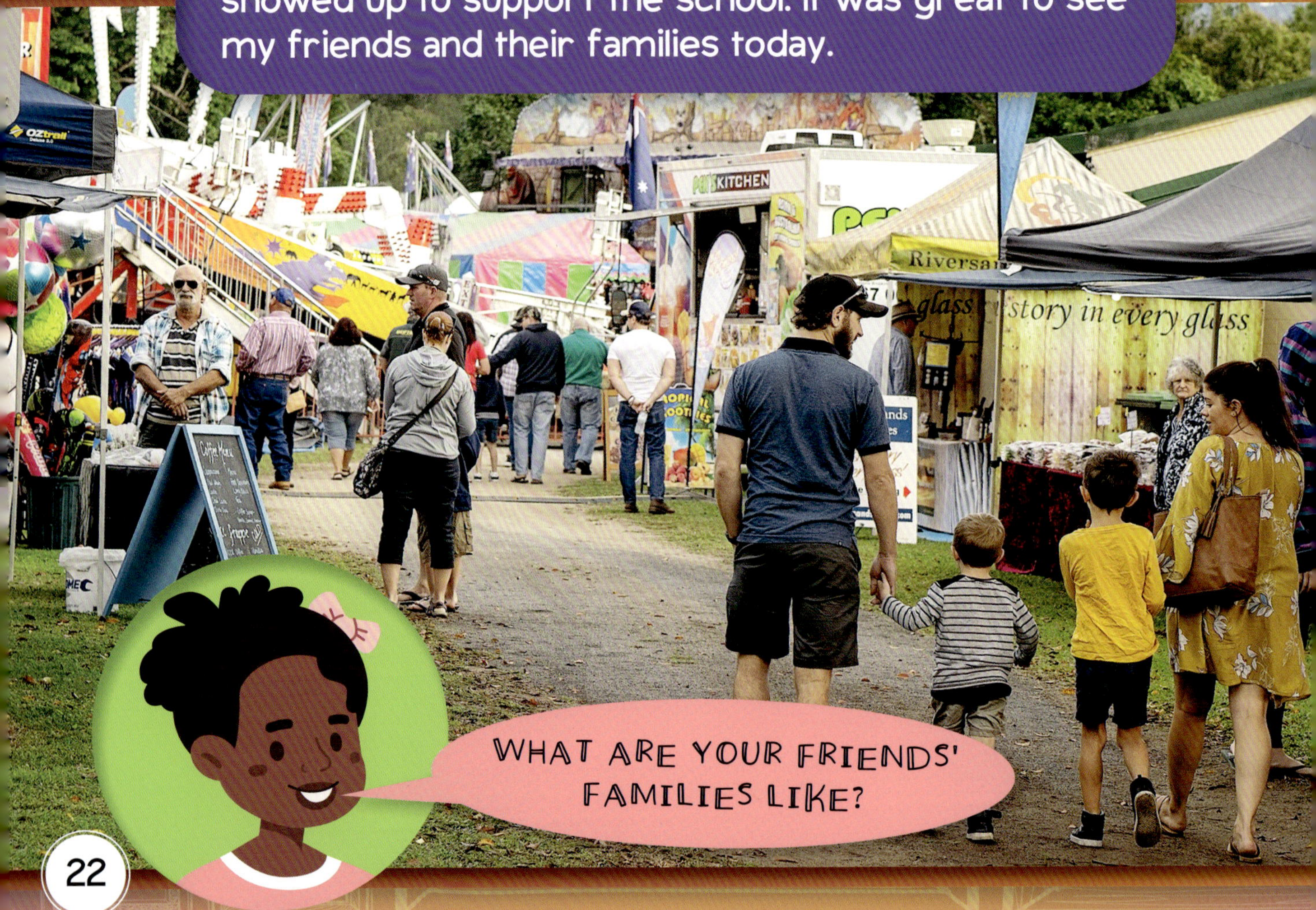

Our families help shape who we are. Each family is unique. However, they all have one thing in common. They are filled with people who love one another.

GLOSSARY

ancestry	relatives who lived a long time ago
bond	a relationship based on love, friendship, or loyalty
Hindu	people who follow a religion called Hinduism, which features many gods
legal	recognised by the law
pregnant	when someone has one or more babies growing inside them
ritual	an ordered action that takes place during a religious ceremony
unique	unlike anything or anyone else

INDEX